STEP-BY-STE

DRAWING&
PAINTING

Hilary Devonshire
and
Henry Pluckrose

Photography: Chris Fairclough

FRANKLIN WATTS
London/New York/Sydney/Toronto

Copyright © 1990
Franklin Watts

Franklin Watts
96 Leonard Street
London EC2A 4RH

Franklin Watts Australia
14 Mars Road
Lane Cove
N.S.W. 2066

UK ISBN: 0 7496 0228 7

Design: Edward Kinsey
Editor: Jenny Wood
Printed in Belgium

The authors wish to
record their thanks in
the preparation of this
book to: Chris Fairclough
for the excellence of his
step-by-step
photographs; Chester
Fisher, Franklin Watts
Ltd, for his advice and
guidance; and all the
young people whose
work they drew upon to
illustrate this book.

The following
photographs are
reproduced by
permission of the
Electricity Council: 12 on
page 24, 13 on page 24
and 3 on page 27.

The following
photographs were taken
by Henry Pluckrose: 5 on
page 10, 6 on page 10, 6
on page 15, 16 on page
26 and 8 on page 30.

Contents

SECTION ONE:

DRAWING

Equipment and materials

Section One: Drawing describes activities which use the following:

Apron (or old shirt)
Candles (white)
Canvas (small piece)
Card
Chalks
Charcoal
Cold water dyes
Crayons
Eraser (soft rubber)
Fixative, and mouth spray
  diffuser
Glue
Graphite
Inks — drawing inks
    — waterproof ink
Knife
Knitting needle
Magazine
Modelling clay
Natural objects (e.g. an apple,
  a flower, a leaf)
Newspaper
Paintbrush
Paints — poster colours
    — watercolours

Paper — cartridge paper
    — sketch pads
    — sugar or construction
      paper
    — typing paper
Paper doily
Paper tissues
Pastels — chalk pastels
    — oil pastels
    — soft pastels
Pencil sharpener
Pencils (varying grades)
Pens — cartridge pens
    — felt-tip pens
    — fibre-tip pens
    — fountain pens
Printing roller
Ruler
Saucer (old)
Scissors
Sponge (small piece)
Stick (thin)
Sticky tape
Water, and water jar
Water soluble colours — crayons
            — pastels
            — pencils

Drawing is the art of creating a picture or design by making lines on a surface with a pen, pencil, or other mark-making instrument. Having a variety of crayons, pencils and sheets of paper in front of you, all ready to use, is exciting. It encourages you to want to make a picture.

What will you draw? To develop your skill, you need to practise drawing different sorts of subjects – buildings, people, landscapes, or things from nature such as animals, birds and plants. You may want to try quick sketches, or you may prefer to work slowly and carefully, studying your subject in detail.

Some hints

Keep your pencils, pencil sharpener and rubbers in a pencil case or tin. Other drawing materials such as crayons, charcoals, inks and pens, can be stored in a large box.

Remember that there are many types of paper. Some are smooth and shiny, others have rougher surfaces. As you work, you will discover how each type can create a different effect.

For some of the later activities where you work with inks or paint, you will need an apron or old shirt to protect your clothes. When you work 'wet' you will also need to cover your working surface with newspaper or a plastic sheet.

The activities in Section One are designed to encourage you to explore the art of drawing. We suggest ways in which you can experiment with a range of materials, for it is through exploration that you will come to understand how the various materials and equipment behave. We hope, too, that as you work through the ideas, you will discover the delights and pleasures of drawing.

drawing with wax crayons

Wax crayons are fun to work with. They are made in a wide range of sizes and colours. They can be sharpened to a point for line work or used flat on their side to give broad strokes.

You will need different coloured wax crayons and a selection of paper.

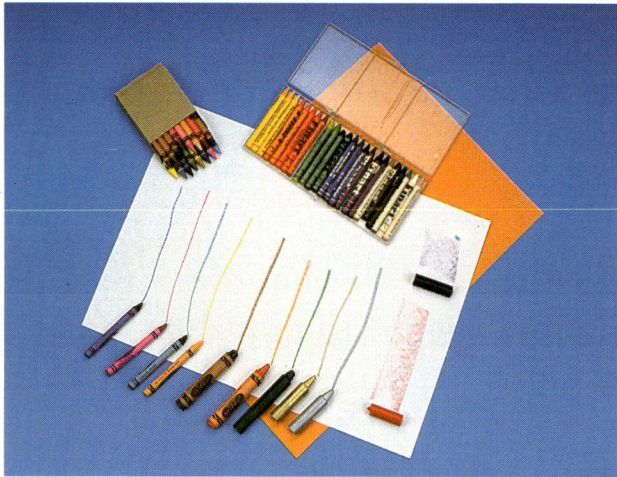

1 Different crayons give different effects.

Try to make a picture using only lines. You can make a fine line by pressing lightly, or you can press hard for strong, heavy colour. Experiment with just one coloured crayon on coloured paper.

2 Draw a picture in lines, using a thin crayon.

3 Add further lines in different colours to complete the design. Notice that the picture is made up of lines only. It has not been coloured in.

4 *The Discovery* A white line drawing on a blue background.

Careful observation can develop your sense of distance. The art of drawing a picture so that you give an impression of distance is called perspective.

5 *'Church Interior'*

6 *'Village Street'*

You will need a selection of pencils, paper, a rubber, and a pencil sharpener or knife.

Pencils are graded according to the hardness or softness of the graphite they contain. The most common is the medium grade HB. Softer pencils are graded from B to 7B (the softest), and harder pencils from H to 7H (the hardest). You can buy pencils in a wide range of colours.

Rough, grainy papers, such as cartridge paper, provide a good surface for pencil work. Smooth papers can be used for the softer leads. Sketch pads are useful for outdoors and for making a collection of sketches.

1 Equipment for drawing with pencils.

2 A selection of papers for drawing. Notice that sketch pads are included.

When you draw, always start with a sharp pencil. Pencil sharpeners are safe and easy to use, but pencils sharpened with a knife give a longer point and therefore stay sharper for a greater length of time.

3 Make a stroke with each of your pencils, to test their grades. Does pressing harder make a difference? The flat pencils here are grades B, 2B and 4B.

4 Experiment with a flat pencil to make different shapes and patterns.

Tones are different shades of grey and black. You can make tones with lines, dots and other patterns. Crossed lines are called cross-hatching. Different tones made in this way can be used in pencil drawing as a means of shading the darker areas.

You will need a selection of pencils and paper.

1 Examples of tones. Make a collection of your own. Experiment with different grades of pencil.

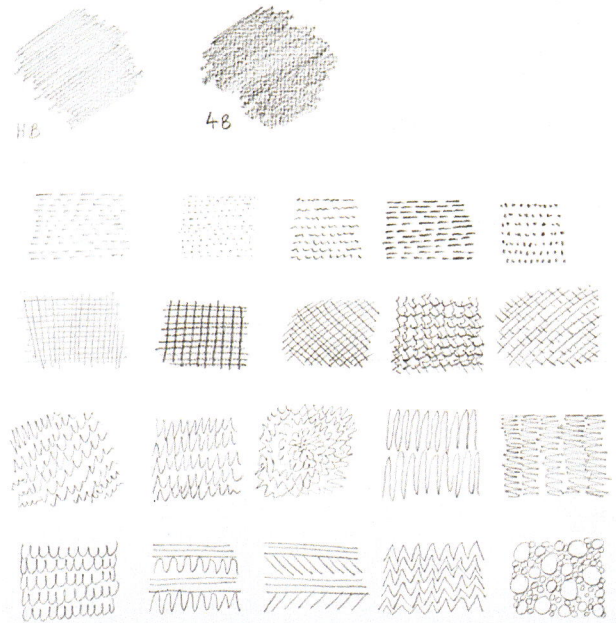

Scribbles, strokes and spirals drawn quickly in freehand can give depth to a flat drawing.

2 Draw some flat shapes on a piece of paper. Place another sheet of thin paper on top. Try to give the shapes body and depth using scribbles, strokes and spirals.

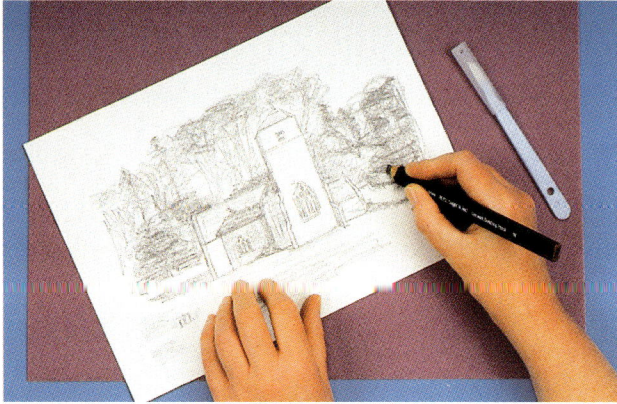

3 *Church* Make a quick sketch using a broad, soft pencil such as a flat 4B.

4 Now make a second picture using a sharply pointed pencil such as an ordinary HB to give finer detail.

5 Here, quick strokes and spirals create a good impression of a battle scene.

6 A head drawn in soft pencil. Can you work out how the different tones have been achieved?

Object drawing

A way of developing your skills is to arrange then draw one or more objects. Look at your arrangement very carefully before you begin.

7 This sketch was done with a graphite pencil followed by coloured pencils. You could use a torch to change the direction of the light and therefore the position of the shadows.

8 *Soldiers* A sketch made using coloured pencils.

A frame made from card can be used like the viewfinder in a camera to help you choose what you want to draw and how you want to draw it. Should your picture be a wide, horizontal shape? (This is known as a *landscape* layout.) Perhaps it would look better as a tall, vertical picture, a *portrait* layout? How much of your subject do you want to show in the picture?

You will need card, a pencil, a ruler, scissors, sticky tape, a stick and modelling clay.

1 A piece of card with a square or rectangular hole makes a useful frame.

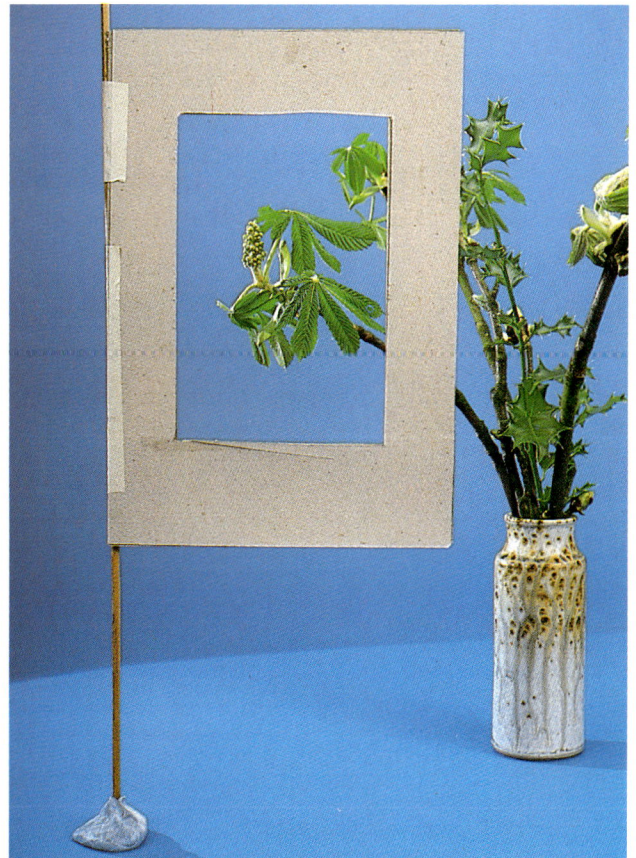

2 Keep your frame in position while you draw by taping it on to a stick held in modelling clay.

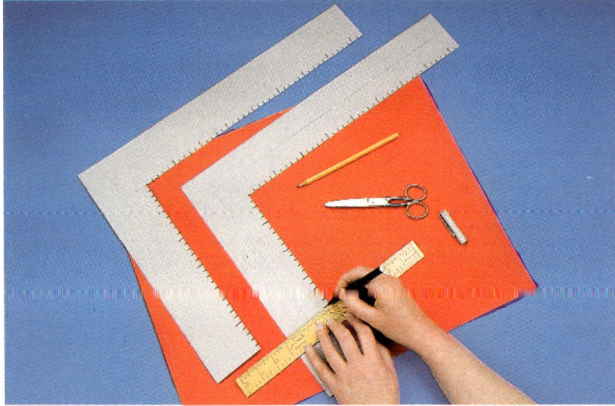

3 Two L-shaped pieces of card will give many shapes and sizes when overlapped. Make small marks on the inside edges of each piece of card, 1cm apart. These marks will act as guides when forming a frame.

4 Find a picture or photograph and use your L-shaped pieces of card to help you choose a section which will be interesting to draw.

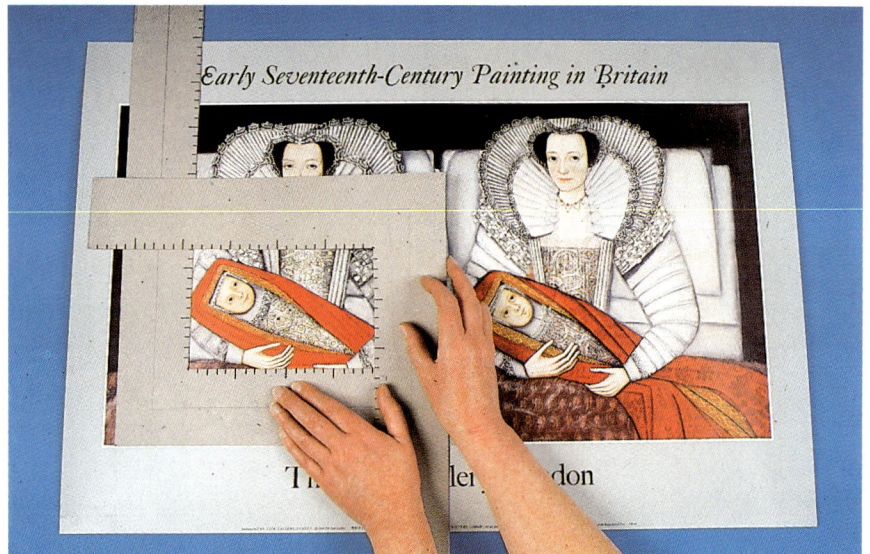

Early Seventeenth-Century Painting in Britain

5 A square makes a good frame for this portrait detail.

6 Two rectangular
frames can also be
used to select the
detail you wish to
copy.

Graphite, chalk and charcoal are all soft materials which blend easily. They can be textured with the fingers or lightened by using a putty rubber. This soft quality means that pictures worked in any of these materials need to be 'fixed' to prevent smudging.

1 A selection of equipment for use when drawing with graphite, chalk and charcoal.

Drawing with graphite
Solid sticks of graphite are like pencils with no wooden casing.

You will need graphite sticks, paper, a paper doily and a knife.

2 A graphite stick on its side will give broad strokes. Use one in this way to take an impression of the paper doily. You could cut and tear your own paper shapes to create a background landscape for a drawing like this.

3 Use the knife to make some graphite powder.

4 Spread the powder with your fingers to start a picture.

5 *Volcano* Add lines to complete the picture.

Making a paper stump

When you are working with graphite, chalks or charcoal, a paper stump is a useful tool. It will prevent your fingers getting dirty and leaving smudgy prints on your picture.

You will need a strip of paper, a knitting needle and sticky tape.

6 To make a paper stump, curl the strip of paper round the knitting needle.

7 Pull the knitting needle away and tighten one end of the stump to a point. Fasten the stump with tape so that it does not unroll.

Drawing with chalks

Chalks can be obtained in a range of colours. They smudge easily, and different colours can be blended by rubbing gently with your finger or with a paper stump. When your picture is finished, spray it with fixative to prevent smudging.

You will need a selection of chalks, paper, a paper stump, and a mouth spray diffuser and fixative.

8 First draw your picture in chalk.

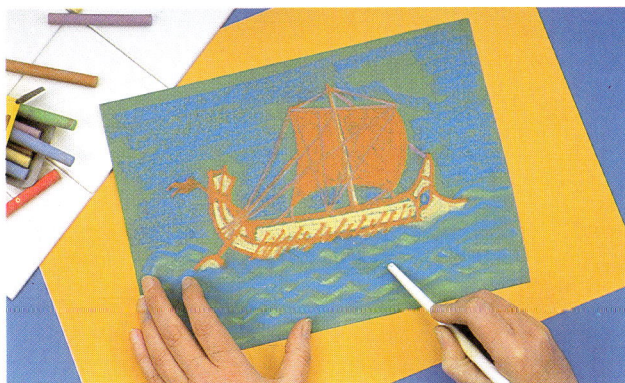

9 Using the paper stump, experiment with blending some of the colours.

10 Fix your design using the mouth spray diffuser and fixative.

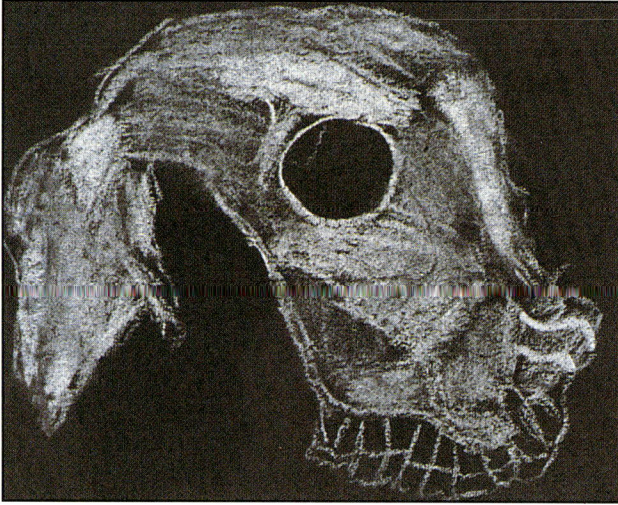

11 *Skull* White chalk is effective on a black background.

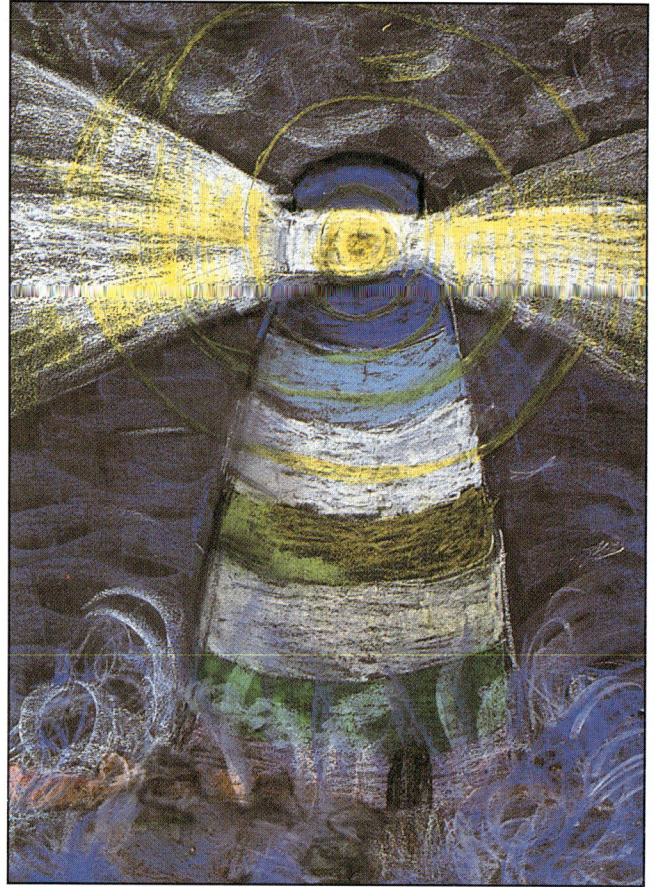

12 *Lighthouse* This picture was made with coloured chalks on a blue background.

13 *Iron* Can you find a household object which would be interesting to draw?

Drawing with charcoal

Charcoal (charred wood) was the first drawing material used by humans. In prehistoric times it was used to draw the outlines of animals on cave walls.

Nowadays, sticks of charcoal are made by burning thin twigs slowly in special kilns.

As well as the common black charcoal, you can also buy charcoals in a range of greys.

You will need a selection of charcoal, paper, chalk and a paper stump.

14 Experiment with different shades of grey. If you do not have special grey charcoals, try blending your black charcoal with white chalk.

15 Using a charcoal stick, draw an outline of your picture. Colour it with charcoal and chalk. Smudge some areas with the paper stump for special effect.

16 *Troll* The finished picture.

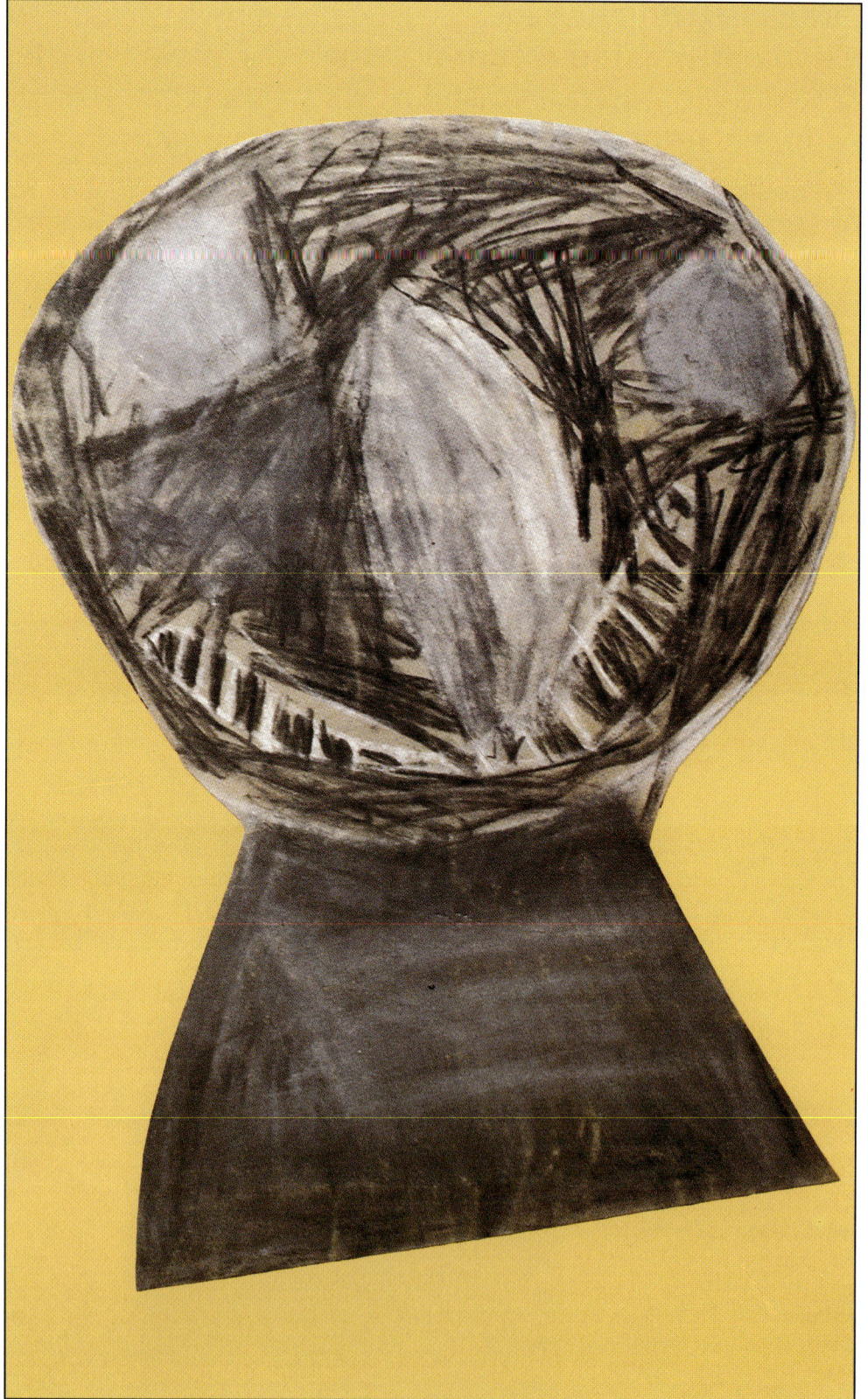

There are several different types of pastel. Some are chalky, others are soft and easy to handle. Oil pastels blend together easily. As you experiment with different pastels you will learn how they behave. Try working on tinted papers, or on paper with a rough, grainy surface such as cartridge papers.

You will need soft pastels, paper and a flower or leaf.

1 Using your soft pastels, lay down some areas of colour side by side. Use four or five different colours and rub gently with your finger to blend them together.

2 Carefully copy the colours from the flower or leaf. Can you mix your pastels to the right shades?

3 *Drying My Hair* A self portrait worked in pastel.

Camouflaging a square

This idea shows how versatile pastels can be. Every colour can be created from one set of oil pastels if they are mixed together very carefully.

You will need oil pastels, a small piece of card or a blank postcard, a pencil, a ruler, scissors, an old magazine, paper and glue.

4 First cut a hole 5cm square in the centre of the piece of card or postcard. Find a coloured picture in the magazine and use your 'viewfinder' frame (see page 17) to select an interesting section. Choose a section with a variety of colours around the edges.

5 Cut out the picture section and paste it on to the centre of a sheet of paper.

6 Using your oil pastels, work out from the edges of the picture section, trying to match the colour tones exactly. You will need to work carefully to blend the right colours. Sometimes you may need to mix two or three colours together.

7 The finished picture. Can you see the camouflaged square?

8 *Crowd Scene* A
picture made with oil
pastels.

Long ago, monks used pens to write and illustrate their books. These pens were usually quill pens made from goose feathers, and the monks wrote on skins from sheep or goats.

Nowadays there are many types of pen: fountain pens and cartridge pens which hold their own ink, dip pens for use with bottles of ink, and many types of fibre- and felt-tip pens. The different pens vary greatly in size.

You will need to try out your pens to see if they give a broad, wide line, or a fine, narrow line.

Drawing inks are supplied in a range of colours. Some inks can be diluted with water. Some, such as Indian ink, are waterproof. When working with pens and inks, it is best to work on fairly strong, smooth paper.

You will need a selection of pens, inks and paper.

1 A selection of materials for drawing with pen and ink.

2 Make a collection of lines to test your pens. Which pens make a very fine line?

3 Try sketching with a fine tipped pen. You can vary the tones in your shading using dots, lines and cross-hatching, just as you did in your pencil sketches.

4 Try colouring a picture using only lines.

5 *Native Warrior* This was done by a 5-year-old, using a felt-tip pen.

6 *Falcon* A fibre-tip pen design. How many animals can you see?

7 *Into Battle* This too was drawn with felt-tip pens.

8 Monks often decorated the first letter of a new piece of text. You could choose a letter and try to decorate it.

It is possible to remove colour using special painting sticks.

1 Colour a shape using a special painting stick.

2 Draw a design using the eraser stick.

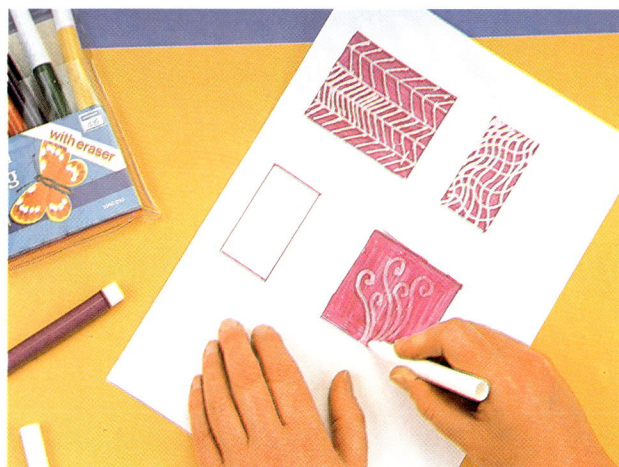

3 Your design will slowly appear as the colour disappears.

4 *Portrait* The white lines and patterns were made by removing colour.

There are a variety of water soluble pencils, crayons and pastels which are fun to use. They can be used both dry and wet, on rough or smooth papers.

You will need a selection of water soluble colours, paper, water and a paintbrush.

1 Some water soluble colours: water soluble pencils (top), painting crayons (centre), painting pastels (bottom).

2 Test your colours to see how they blend together when you wet them with the paintbrush.

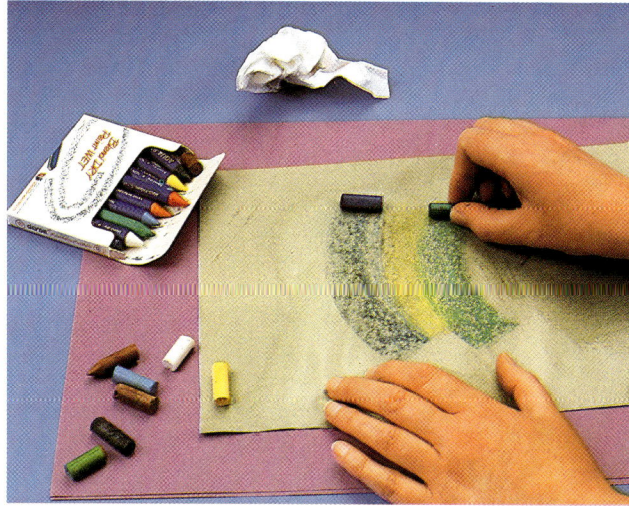

3 Try working on wet paper. Use a painting pastel on its side to prepare a background for a drawing.

4 Alternatively, colour the background with pastels and soften the colours with a wet brush.

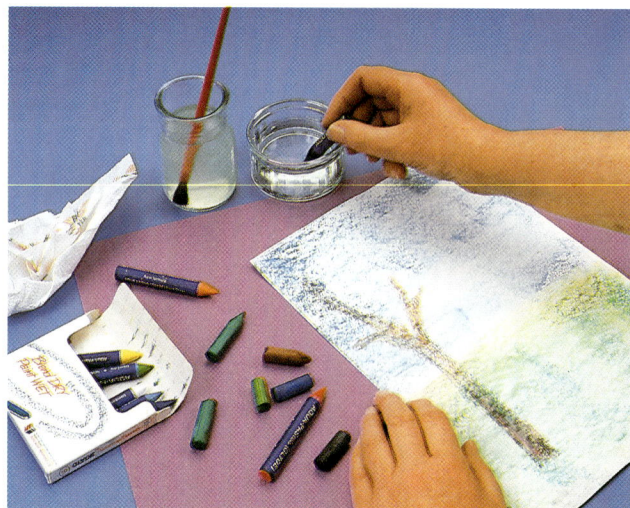

5 Draw a picture using a water soluble pencil, crayon or pastel dipped in water.

6 *Trees* The finished picture.

You will need waterproof ink, a
pen or brush, paper, watercolour
paints and a paintbrush.

1 Draw a picture on smooth
paper using waterproof ink
and the pen or brush.

2 *When the ink is dry,*
colour your picture
with watercolour
paints. The ink can
help to stop the
colours running
together.

3 *Waterfront* The finished picture.

4 Here cold water dyes were used, and the colours allowed to blend together.

Many drawings are made more interesting by being worked on a textured background. You may, for example, like to tint your own paper using a watercolour wash. On a rough weave paper, using a pastel on its side gives an interesting effect.

You can also create different textures by *removing* colour. Use different types of material to do this. Try making a sample sheet of the various effects you achieve.

You will need watercolour paints, a paintbrush, water, an old saucer, paper, paper tissues, a piece of canvas, a sponge and a printing roller.

1 Paint a small area of a sheet of paper with watercolour.

2 Remove some of the colour by pressing down on it with a crumpled paper tissue. Make a print elsewhere on the paper with the paint-covered tissue.

3 Experiment using different materials to give you new textures. Here a piece of canvas and a sponge have been used.

4 Use a printing roller to create a background.

5 Your background may give you an idea for a picture. Could you draw people on the blue mountains?

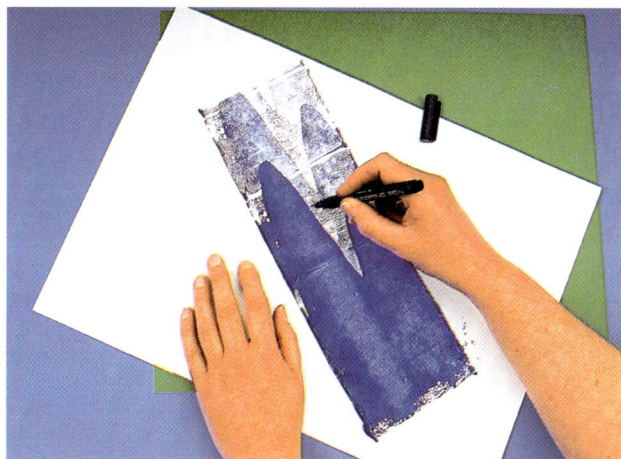

6 Working on a sponge-textured background.

On your own

By now you will have experimented with a variety of techniques. You will have worked with many materials, and discovered how they behave with different types of papers and textured surfaces. Here are a few more ideas for you to try. Have fun!

1 Make a picture which combines two or more of the ideas from pages 8-43. For example, you could draw with inks on a surface prepared with soluble crayons. Or you could make a crayon drawing and wash over your picture with diluted ink.

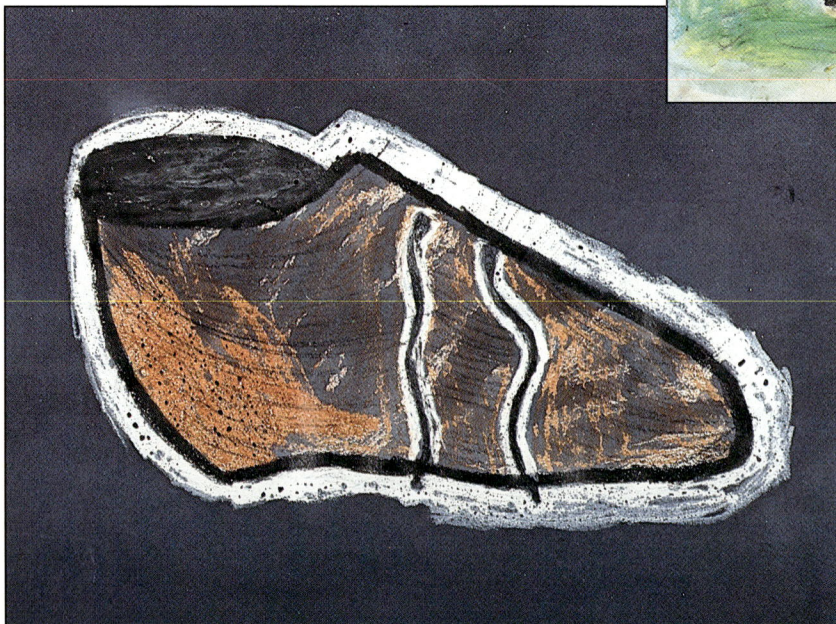

1 *On The Farm* This picture was made using watercolours and felt-tip pens.

2 *Roman Shoe* This sketch of an object in a museum was done with wax crayons and a black ink wash.

2 Make a pencil sketch to use as a foundation for a painting. If you are sketching outdoors, make a note of the colours as you work.

3 *The Cutty Sark* A pencil sketch.

4 The finished picture, using acrylic paints.

5 *My Bike* This effect was achieved by using poster paint over a pencil drawing.

Candle drawings

For this idea you need a white candle, paper, some coloured drawing ink, an old saucer and a paintbrush.

6 Draw a picture with the wax candle.

7 Brush ink over your drawing.

8 The wax of the candle resists the ink and your picture appears through the ink wash.

Drawing with hot candle wax
ASK AN ADULT TO HELP WITH THIS.

Make a drawing using melted candle wax which has been heated in an old saucepan. Work on a table covered with plenty of old newspaper, and be careful not to spill any wax. Use inks or cold water dyes to colour your picture. When you have finished, remove the wax by ironing your picture through several sheets of newspaper.

9 *Indian Chief* A candle wax drawing created from a museum sketch.

3 Make a book of sketches.

10 Your sketches could include illustrations for a story, copies of interesting objects in a museum, or scenes from a holiday.

SECTION TWO:

PAINTING

Equipment and materials

Section Two: Painting describes activities which use the following:

This book describes activities which use the following:

Acrylic (PVA) medium

Card

Charcoal

Clear furniture polish

Cold water paste

Drinking straws

Gravel (or fine sand)

Indian ink

Jam jars (old) for water

Knitted glove (old)

Large water bowl or tray

Lino printing roller (or household paint roller)

Liquid detergent

Marbling colours

Mixing trays

Paint – must be water-based – can be bought as:

(a) powder colour;

(b) tempera blocks;

(c) small bricks or tubes of artists' water colour;

(d) tubes of acrylic colour (PVA);

(e) finger paints;

(f) poster colours;

(g) texture colours;

(h) tempera paste.

Make sure you buy at least these five basic colours: red, yellow, blue, black and white.

Paintbrushes (varying sizes and types)

Palette knife

Paper – cartridge, sugar or construction paper

Paper clips

Pencil

Saucer or plate

Scissors

Scrap material – e.g. pieces of bark, braid, buttons, card, cotton, fur, hair, lace, leather, matchsticks, newspaper and paper scraps of all kinds, paper plates, paper tissues, plastic, raffia, ribbon, sacking, sequins, shells, small stones, sponges, twigs, small pieces of wood, wool

Tablespoon

Texture paste (for use with acrylic colours)

Water

Section Two has been prepared to encourage you to experiment with colour. The activities and ideas outlined here will help you to discover how particular types of paints behave, the many different ways in which colour can be applied and the kinds of surfaces which are suitable for picture-making.

There is no one way to paint a picture. All artists experiment with colour, shape, pattern and texture. Each uses materials in a personal way.

Once you have learned how materials behave, experiment for yourself. To be creative is not just following instructions. The creative person takes an idea and turns it into something which is his or her own.

Some hints

Before you begin, remember that art activities can be messy!

If you are using this book at home, take all the precautions you would take at school. Cover the table with newspaper and the floor around it with an old cotton sheet or a piece of plastic sheeting (e.g. a large dustbin liner).

Cover yourself too. An old shirt or blouse, particularly if it is too big, will give you excellent protection from top to toe.

1 Water-based paints are sold in many different packagings. Always read the instructions before you begin.

Your paint

How you use paint will depend upon the type of paint you have. All of the paint colours mentioned in this book are water-based. This means that, to work with them, you will need water.

(a) Powder colour is in powder form and has to be mixed with a wetting agent (e.g. water, liquid detergent) before it can be used. Always add water to powder – never powder to water.

(b) Tempera blocks are solid blocks of colour. The surface of each block needs to be thoroughly dampened before use.

(c) Artists' water colour is sold in small bricks and in tubes. It can be expensive.

(d) Acrylic colour (PVA) is a thick creamy paint, usually sold in large tubes. Acrylic colours have a plastic base and can be thinned with water. Particular care has to be taken when using acrylic paint as its base is also a strong adhesive (glue). When not being used (even for a short period), paintbrushes must be cleaned or kept in water. If this is not done, the brush heads will dry solid. (You can make your own acrylic colours by mixing powder colour with acrylic medium – see pages 77-78.)

2 Colour can be applied in many ways. Notice the range of brush heads.

3 Palettes like these are useful when working with acrylic colour.

4 Bun and cake trays make excellent palettes.

(e) Finger paint colours have been specially prepared for painting with the hands. (You can make your own finger paint mix by mixing water paste and powder colour – see page 93.)

(f) You can use other kinds of water-based paints (e.g. poster colours, texture colours, tempera paste). Oil-based paints are not suitable for the activities described in this book, except for those on pages 74-76.

Your brushes
Brushes are sold by size. The lower the number (e.g. 2), the smaller the brush. Try to build up a collection of brushes in sizes 2, 4, 6, 8, 10 and 12.

5 Artists' water colour, palette and brushes.

Some brushes are made with a 'flat' tip, some are shaped to a point. Build up a range of brush types.

Brushes are made in different materials. Some (like squirrel hair and sable) are very soft. Others (like hog hair) are hard. Some are made with synthetic materials.

Remember – no one brush is suitable for every activity!

Your paper

Pictures can be painted on almost any kind of paper. The type of paper (or 'support') chosen will depend upon the type of paint being used. For example, thin tissue paper would not be a very suitable 'support' for heavy layers of acrylic paint.

6 Build up a stock of paper of different types and colours. Try to select a paper for your painting which links to the subject.

Finger paintings can be worked with thick pre-mixed paints on almost any type of paper. The most important thing to remember when using finger paint is to work quickly. Marks can be drawn into the paint only while it is wet.

Prints can also be taken from finger paintings.

1 Spread a quantity of finger paint into a clean tray.

2 While the paint is wet, draw a picture into it with the tip of your finger.

3 Place a clean sheet of paper over your picture (the paint must still be wet) and smooth it down with the backs of your hands. Do not press too hard.

4 Pull the paper away carefully. A print or transfer of the picture will now be on the paper. How does the print differ from the original?

5 This picture, if it is still wet, can also be used to give a transfer. Simply place a piece of paper over it, smooth down and peel off.

6 The finger painting (on white paper) and its transfer picture.

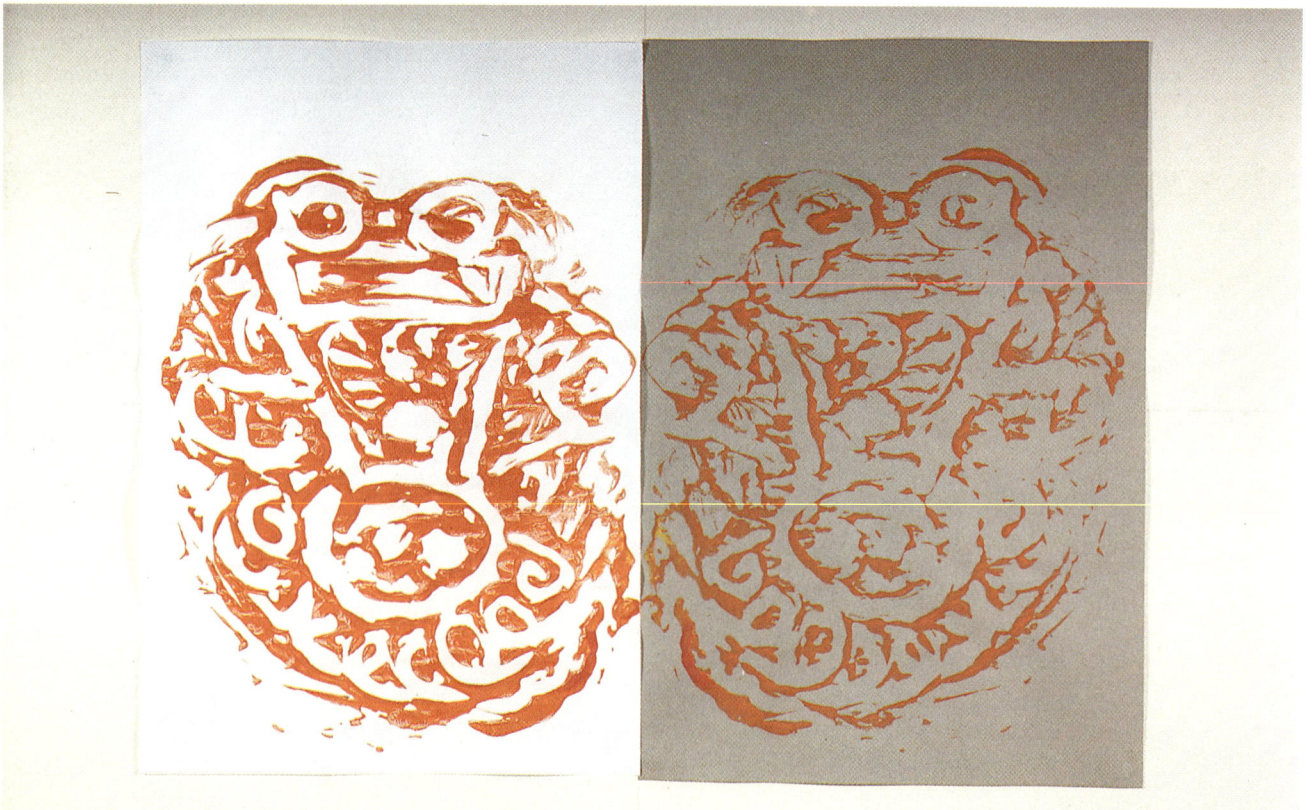

7 *The Scarecrow*
Finger paints can also
be used to make
pictures by painting
with the fingers
directly on to paper.

Colour 'combing'

Finger paint mix can also be used to make attractively patterned paper. When dry, a sheet of colour-combed paper makes an excellent book cover. Before using a sheet of combed paper to cover a book, you will need to 'fix' the colour by rubbing a thin layer of clear furniture polish over the pattern. Make sure the paint is dry first!

1 Make a comb from card by cutting notches along one edge.

2 Spread finger paint mix into a tray. Draw in it with your comb.

3 While the paint is still wet, place a sheet of paper over the design. Smooth it down lightly with the backs of your hands.

4 The combed sheet.

Applying colour with wood

Experiment to discover how different materials make different kinds of marks in wet paint. Would the soft edge of a feather, for example, give the same sort of line as the piece of wood which has been used to draw the knight shown here?

1 Put two spoonfuls of thick colour on to a sheet of paper.

2 Spread the colour evenly over the paper's surface.

3 While the paint is still wet, draw into it with a small piece of wood.

4 *Knight* Why is it important to choose a paper which is a contrasting colour to the paint?

Applying colour with a roller

Another way of applying colour is with a roller. The type shown here is designed for lino printing, but a small household paint roller would do just as well. The roller is used to texture and colour the paper. The texture provides the background for painting.

1 (Above) Squeeze some colour into a tray. Charge the roller with colour and roll it to and fro across the paper.

2 (Below) When the textured paper is dry, paint a design on to it. The design could be made up of simple lines or of blocks of colour.

3 *The Old Chair In Sunlight* Here the textured sheet has been used to provide the background for a silhouette.

4 *At the Concert* Here the silhouettes are in two colours.

5 *The Strange Bird* More than one colour can be used for the textured background.

6 *The Park* Here the roller has been used to paint most of the picture – in shades of green.

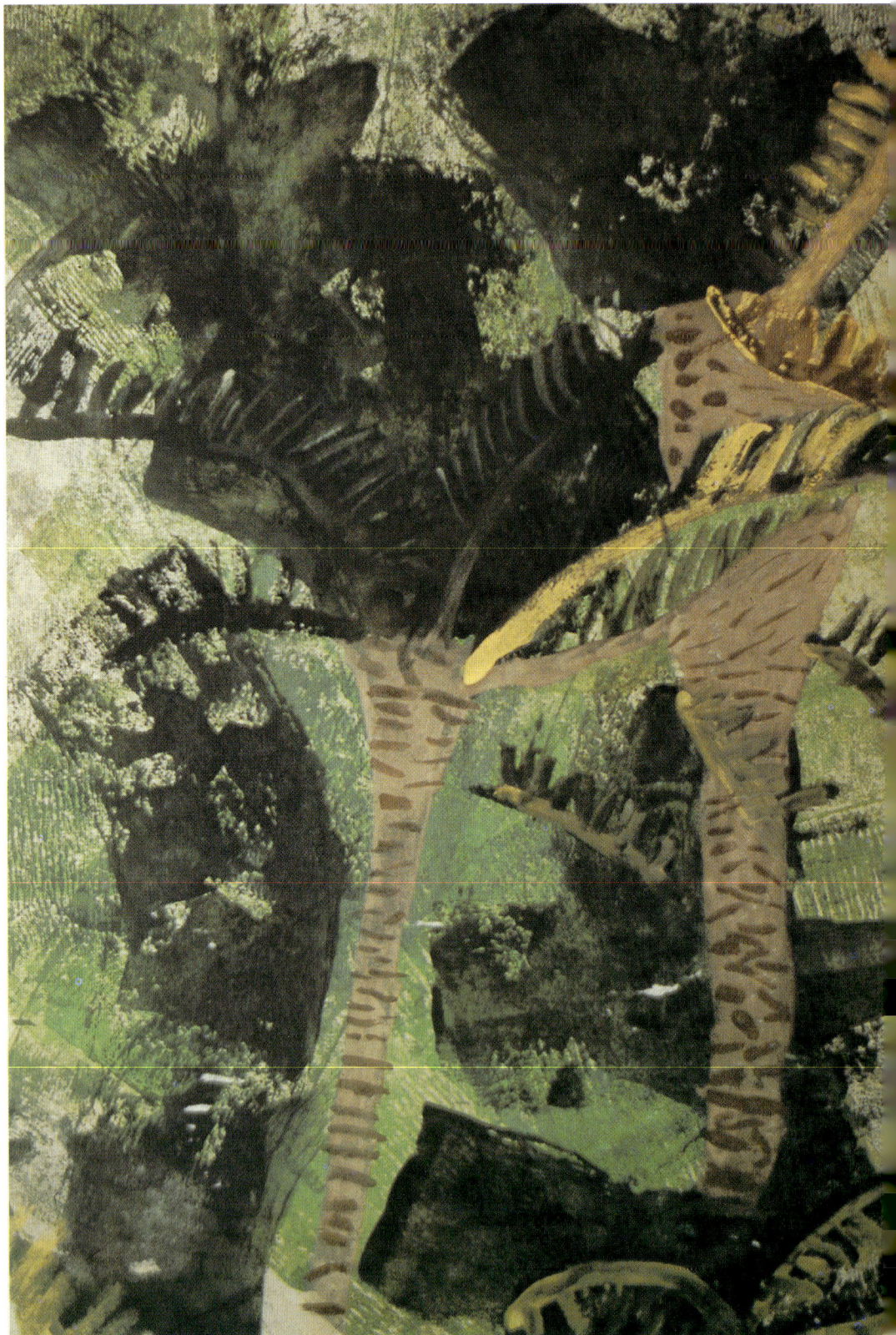

Applying colour with scrap material

Sort your scrap material (see page 50) into several piles. Into one, put all the soft materials (e.g. scraps of wool, fabric, sacking) and into the other all the hard materials (e.g. wood, bark, twigs). Divide each pile into materials which have a heavy surface texture (like bark) and those which have very little (like smooth plastic). Experiment with the materials you have collected to see what kind of 'mark' they make when used to apply colour. Could you make a picture using only soft materials to apply colour? Could you make a picture using only hard materials?

1 A simple way to charge scrap material with colour is to make a colour pad with a piece of sponge. Place the sponge in a saucer and pour paint on to it. Charge the scraps with colour by pressing them into the paint-soaked sponge.

2 *Wild Cat* This picture was painted using a small scrap of sponge to apply the colour.

For this activity you will need an old knitted glove. It is easy to apply colour cleanly and evenly with a glove. Try wrapping other kinds of textured material tightly around one hand. Charge your covered hand with colour and use it to produce a pattern. Vary your pattern by working in different colours.

1 Roll out some colour into a tray.

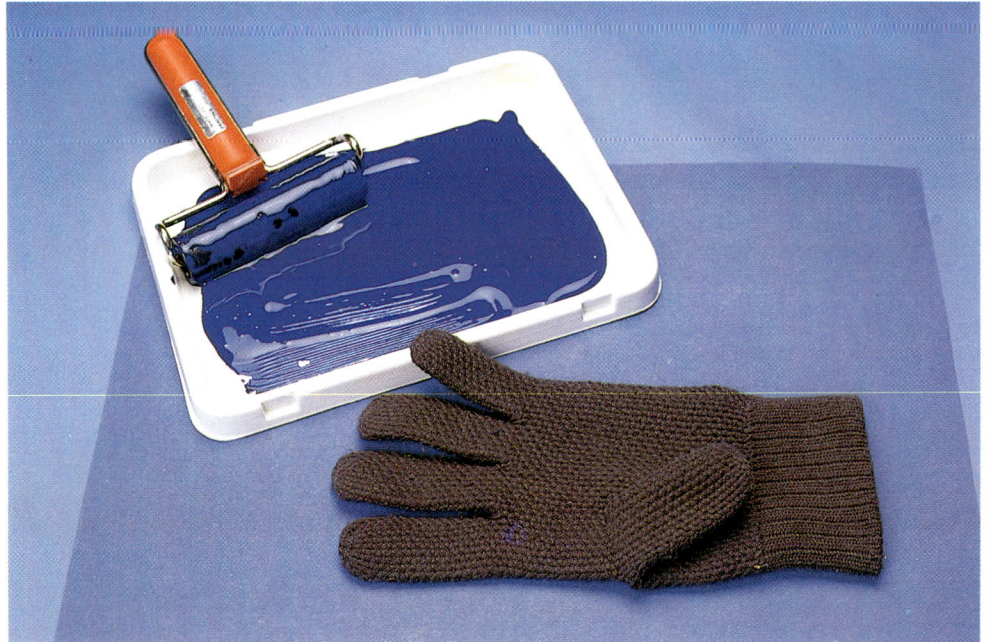

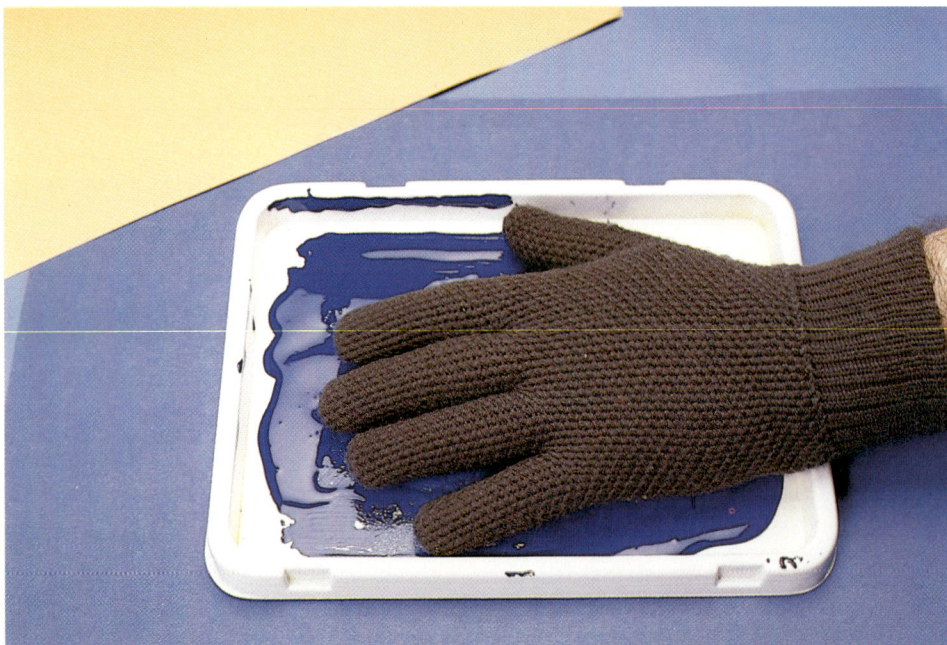

2 Charge the glove with colour.

3 Apply the paint-charged glove to paper.

4 *The Old Glove*
Notice how the paint echoes the texture of the material.

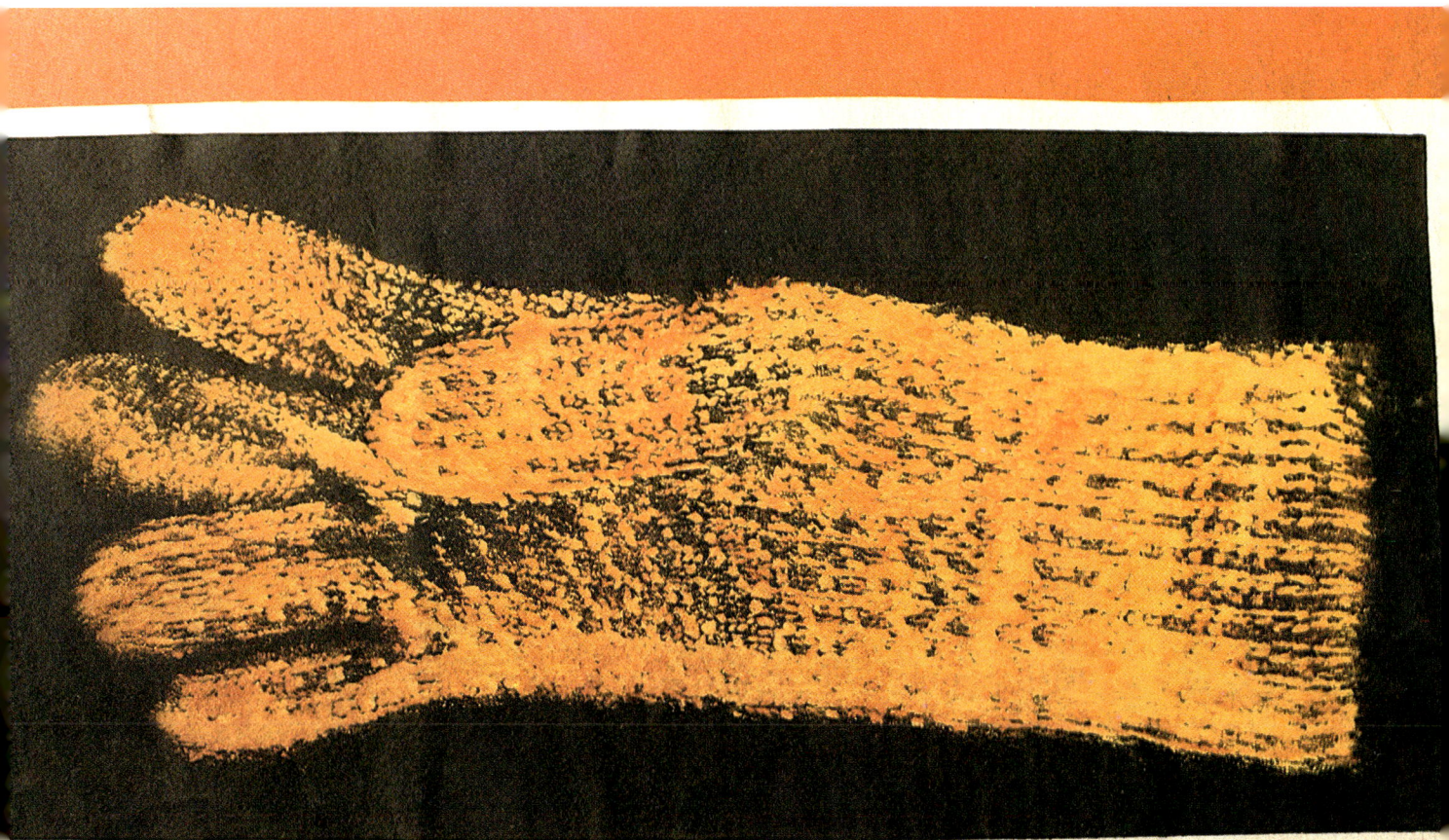

Applying colour with a straw

Pictures can be made by applying colour in tiny dots or spots. A simple way to make a dot picture is to apply the colour with a drinking straw.

1 Place some thick paint into a palette. Here tempera paste has been squeezed on to paper plates – one plate and one straw for each colour. The picture is built up by using the tip of the straw to apply colour.

2 *Church Window* A dot picture painted entirely with drinking straws.

As we have seen, colour can be applied with the surface of a piece of card. It can also be applied with its thin edge.

1 Take a piece of card (a postcard will do well) and fold it against itself to make an interesting shape. Use a paper clip to hold the edges together.

2 Charge the edges with colour and use them to make a pattern or picture.

3 *Trees* You could also
try to make a picture
by applying colour
with the edge of an
unfolded piece of card.

Applying colour in a splatter

It's not even necessary always to use brushes, rollers or other materials to apply colour. It can be fun simply to apply colour in drips and in 'worms' straight from the tube. This is sometimes called 'action painting'.

1 Squeezing out the colour.

2 Adding drips of colour.

3 *Into Space* A splatter
and drip picture.

Marbling

Marbling colours are special oil-based colours. They are used for making patterned papers.

When dry, marbled papers can be used for book covers, shelf and drawer liners, in model-making and even for writing paper.

1 Make sure all the materials are ready and close at hand before you begin. You will need a bowl of cold water, marbling colours, some straws, and sheets of paper on which to work.

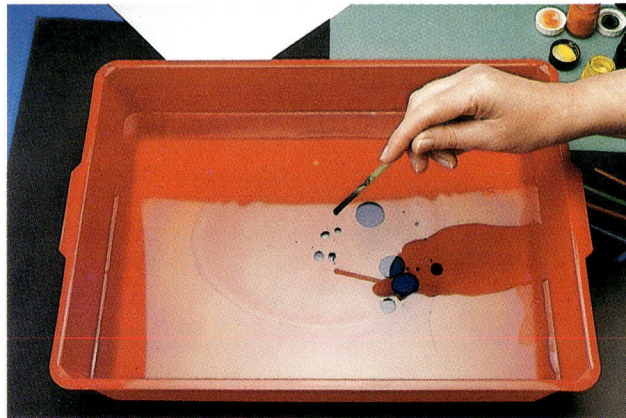

2 Using the tip of a straw, drip a few spots of marbling colour on to the water. Use more than one colour.

3 Stir the surface of the water to make sure that the colour spreads.

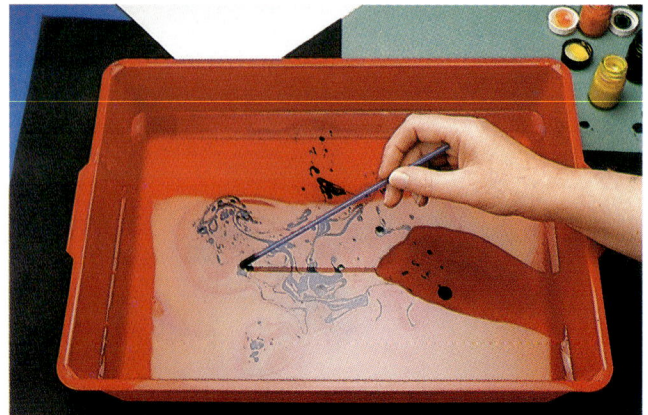

4 Drop a sheet of paper on to the water and leave it to float for a few moments.

5 Remove the paper and leave to dry.

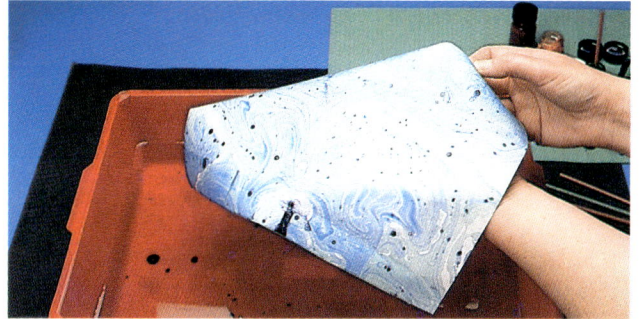

6 A marbled sheet.

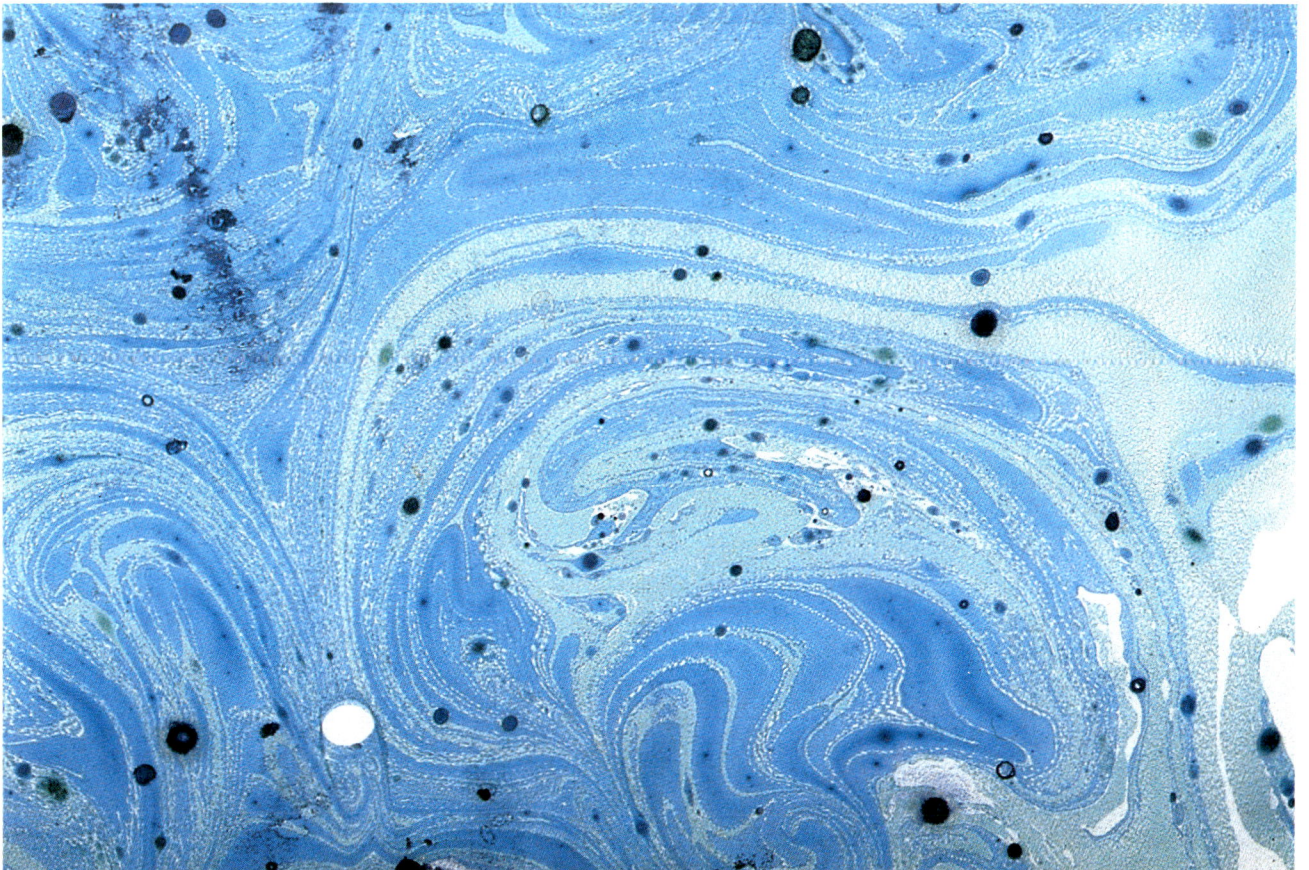

7 *My Friend* Painted
on marbled paper.

Acrylic colour

Acrylic colour is a very thick colour and can be applied with brush, roller or palette knife. But the plastic base can be thinned with cold water, so the colour can also be applied in pale colour washes.

Like all water-based colours, acrylic colours can be mixed with each other on a palette to give new colours and tones.

When making a picture with a thick colour, it is wise to work on heavy paper or thin card.

1 Put one heaped tablespoonful of powder colour into a jar.

2 Slowly add water, stirring the powder until it looks like thick cream.

3 Add PVA medium to the paint and water until the mixture is stiff and difficult to stir.

4 Tip a small quantity of colour on to a palette, and paint – perhaps using a palette knife.

5 (Below) *St Paul's* A knife painting in blue and white acrylic colours. Notice how the colour remains textured when dry.

6 *Strange Face*
A painting on card
in acrylic colours and
using a palette knife,
by a girl of three.

Acrylic texturing

Because acrylic colour is also an adhesive, other materials can be added to it to increase its texture. For example, interesting effects can be obtained by stirring fine sand (or even gravel) into the colour before it is applied to the paper.

Some art suppliers sell extenders and texture pastes to use with acrylic colours.

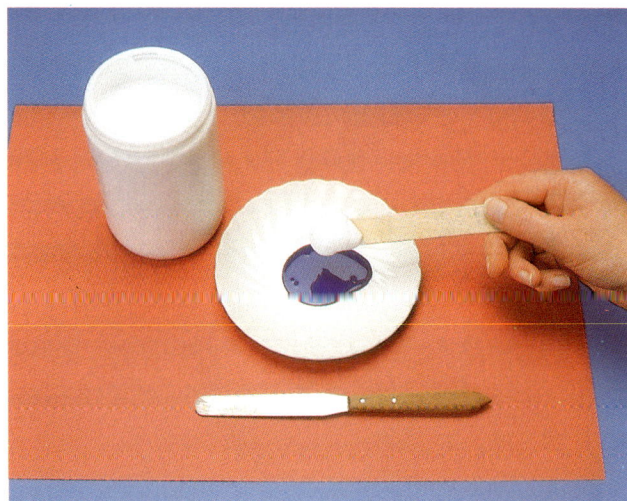

1 (Above) Adding texturing medium to acrylic paint.

2 (Left) Mixing medium and paint together with a palette knife.

3 Painting with a palette knife.

4 (Opposite) *Abstract* A texture painting.

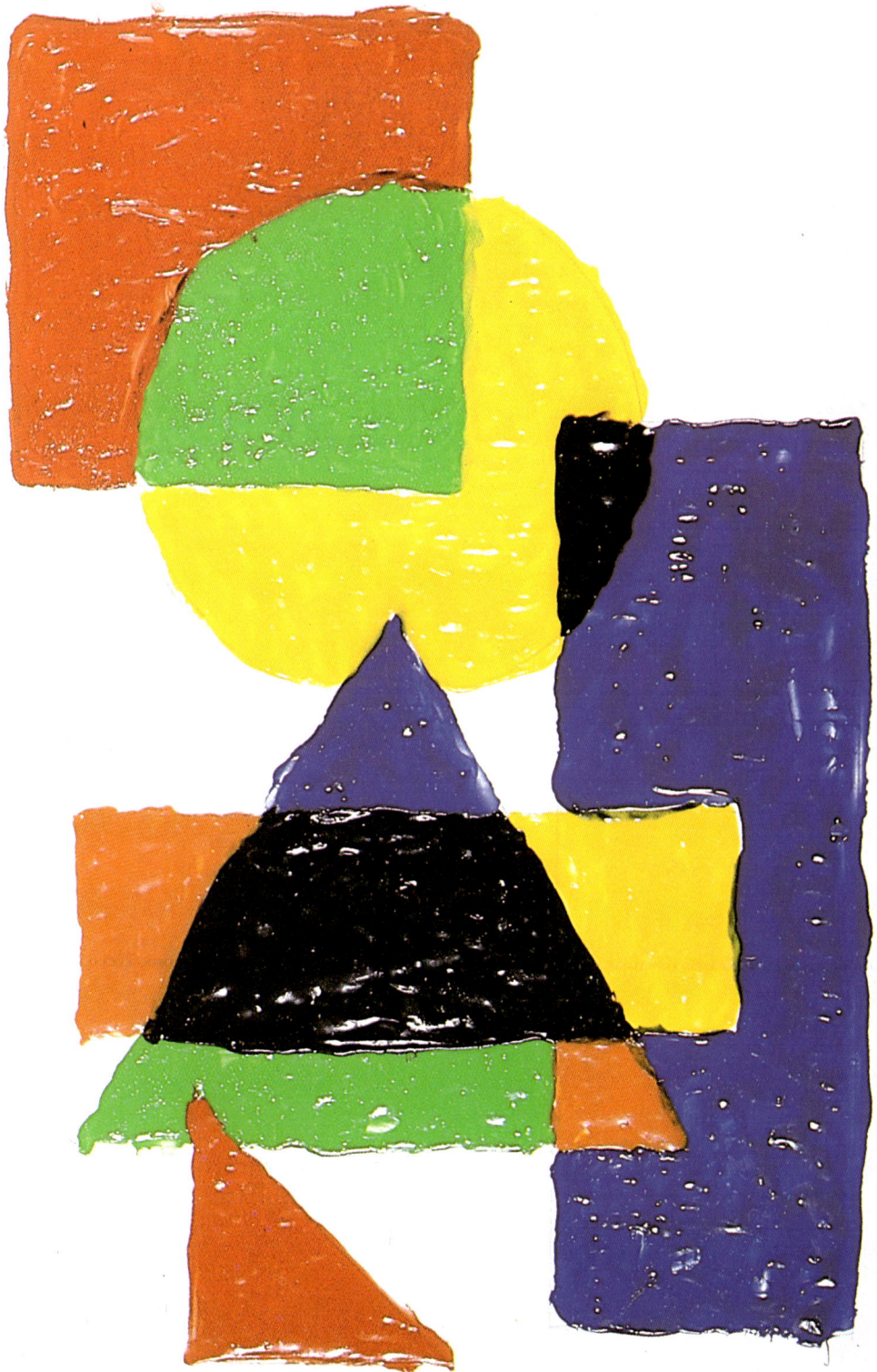

Collage with acrylic colours

A collage is a word used to describe a picture which is made up of scraps of material.

Acrylic colours are also adhesive so if buttons, fabric and paper scraps, matchsticks, sequins, shells, sand or small stones are laid into the paint while it is wet they will stick firmly to it and so become part of the finished picture. The scraps can be given additional texture by overpainting them with acrylic colour.

1 Paint a picture in acrylic colour.

2 While the paint is still wet, add details using scrap material.

4 (Opposite) *The Clown* How many different materials have been used here?

3 Here the collar is being decorated with sequins.

5 *At Sea* Here the picture is made from torn newspaper, a drinking straw and acrylic paint.

6 *A Lion* This picture, painted by a seven-year-old, used cut and torn paper over a thin layer of acrylic colour.

Marbled paper (see pages 74-76) can also be used to make collages. All you need is a selection of marbled paper in different colours. Details can be added in paint.

1 Here a picture of a landscape is being worked. The sheets of marbled paper have been cut into mountain, hill and tree shapes and glued on to a sheet of red paper. Fine details are being added in black paint.

2 *Landscape* A collage in marbled paper.

Using wet paper

Most of the pictures described in Section Two have been worked on dry paper. Working on wet paper produces quite a different result. When paints run together, new, unexpected blends of colour occur.

1 Thoroughly wet the paper with clean water.

2 Apply washes of colour.

3 *Welsh Hillside* A
painting on wet paper
by a nine-year-old.

Bubble patterns

This is another way of patterning paper in an unusual way. The papers produced can be used for book covers and for collage.

1 Squeeze a small quantity of liquid detergent into a jar.

2 Add a spoonful of wet colour (or Indian ink) and mix them together.

3 Blow into the mixture through a drinking straw until bubbles rise over the edge of the jar.

4 Lay a sheet of paper over the bubbles.

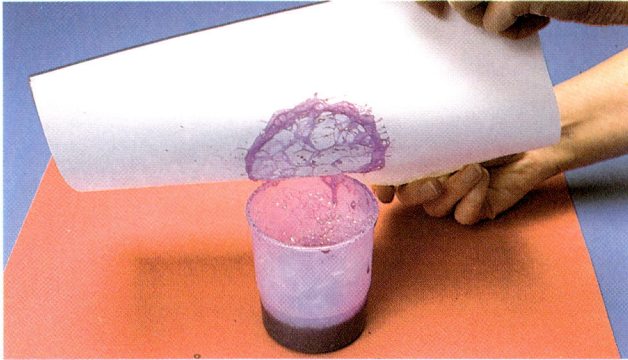

5 The bubble pattern will transfer to the paper.

6 Repeat the process until the whole page is decorated. You could make a pattern in several colours.

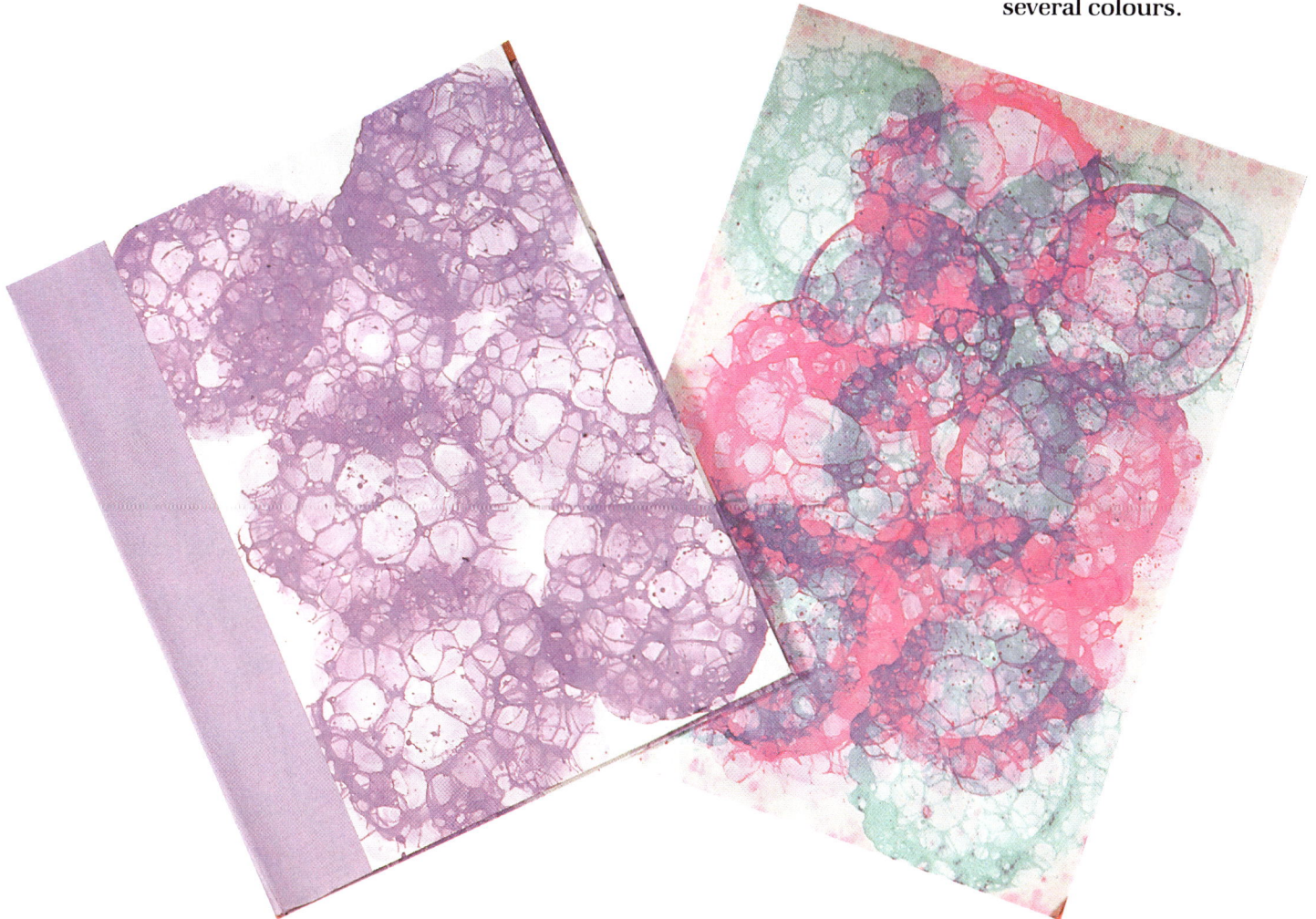

Magic pictures

Indian ink is waterproof. Water-based paint is not. This difference means that these two materials can be used together to produce fascinating pictures.

1 Using water-based paint, draw a picture in lines (i.e. do not fill with colour). Leave to dry.

2 Brush waterproof Indian ink over the painting. Apply the ink thickly but try not to disturb the paint. Leave to dry.

3 Now soak the whole picture in water. With your fingertips, rub the areas you have painted. Because the paint dissolves in water, it will float away, taking with it the covering of Indian ink.

4 When all the paint has been removed, carefully lift the picture from the water. Leave to dry.

On your own

Throughout Section Two you have been experimenting with paints of different kinds. In doing this you will have learned some of the ways in which paints behave. Now try some ideas of your own. Here are some suggestions to help you.

1 Could you make a picture which includes two or more of the ideas contained in pages 55-91? For example, could you use marbled paper for a picture worked in acrylic applied with a palette knife?

2 Could you make a picture applying dry powder colour directly on to wet paper? What happens to the colour? How easy is it to control?

3 Experiment by using a technique of your choice on different types of paper. For example, the effect achieved by applying watercolour washes to pastel paper is very different to that achieved by applying watercolour washes to cartridge paper.

4 Try different types of colour for marbling. What is the effect of laying yellow pastel paper in a tray of orange marbling colours?

5 Experiment by using unusual 'supports' (painting surfaces). For example, you could try making pictures on tissue paper, corrugated card, crêpe paper, newsprint, chipboard. How does the painting surface affect your picture, in the way you apply colour and in the paints you use?

6 Use acrylic paint or thick poster colour to decorate and pattern pebbles and smooth stones. Find some oval-shaped pebbles and decorate them with strange faces … or turn them into weird animals and birds. Acrylic colours are excellent for painting on stone. If you use poster colour, protect the design by applying a final coat of thin varnish. Do this when the paint has dried hard!

7 Look in an encyclopaedia for information about Newton's colour wheel. Make a wheel of your own. What does this teach you about colour?

8 Try painting pictures and patterns using a restricted range of colours e.g. blue and white; white and black; red and yellow; blue and yellow; red and blue.

Most of the materials mentioned in this book are easy to obtain. Many stationers stock a range of paper, a selection of pencils, pens and inks, and a range of art materials such as brushes, papers and paints. Some have an art department in which you can buy specialist materials such as acrylic medium and texture paste.

Other specialist materials such as graphite sticks, broad pencils, pastels, inks and watercolours can be obtained from an artists' materials stockist or ordered through a school supplier such as E J Arnold & Son Ltd, Parkside Lane, Dewsbury Road, Leeds, LS11 5TD.

A useful guide to the stationers and artists' colourmen (shops which sell artists' materials) can be found in *Yellow Pages* and in the Thompson's directory for your area. (Look under 'Art and Craft', 'Artists' Materials' and 'Graphic Arts materials'.)

Acrylic additives
Additives are used to give texture to acrylic colour. They are sold under a brand name (e.g. Polytex). Each additive will be made to a slightly different recipe. Always read the instructions before you begin.

Acrylic colours and medium
All of the major artists' colourmen (e.g. Reeves) manufacture their own range of acrylic colours.

Acrylic medium (for mixing with powder colour to produce an acrylic paint) can be purchased (at very little cost) in small jars. If the medium is being used for a group activity it is economic to buy it in 1- or 5-litre containers.

When dry, most acrylic medium (PVA) forms a waterproof skin. However, a range of PVA which will wash from clothing (e.g. E J Arnold's 'Easy Clean') has been introduced recently.

Finger paint
Finger paint can be made by mixing water paste and powder colour. Add water to two tablespoonsful of powder colour until a thick cream is formed. In a separate jar, mix two tablespoonsful of cold water paste with water until a thick

smooth cream is formed. Now pour the colour on to the paste and stir thoroughly. If the mixture is too thick, add a little water. If it is too thin, stir in dry colour to thicken the mixture.

Fixatives

Fixatives are available for fixing pictures which have been made with soft materials such as pastels and chalk. A mouth spray diffuser is recommended for use with fixatives. Alternatively, hair spray can be used, although it is best to experiment on a small sample of work first to make sure the spray does not cause discolouring.

PRINTED IN BELGIUM BY
proost
INTERNATIONAL BOOK PRODUCTION

Take leaf rubbings using foil & fingers